RUSTIC FIREPLACES

WRITTEN AND PHOTOGRAPHED BY
RALPH KYLLOE

Gibbs Smith, Publisher
TO ENRICH AND INSPIRE HUMANKIND

Salt Lake City | Charleston | Santa Fe | Santa Barbara

For my stepfather, Albert N. Backus

First Edition
11 10 09 08 07   5 4 3 2 1

Text © 2006 Ralph Kylloe
Photographs © 2006 Ralph Kylloe, except as noted.

Published by
Gibbs Smith, Publisher
P.O. Box 667
Layton, Utah 84041

Orders: 1.800.748.5439
www.gibbs-smith.com

Designed by Adrienne Pollard
Printed and bound in China

Library of Congress Control Number: 2006930882

ISBN 13: 978-1-4236-0166-1
ISBN 10: 1-4236-0166-1

This is always the hardest page for me to write. There are many people to thank for their help and assistance with this book. In truth, most of the photos in this book were culled from my archives. Some of the photos appearing here have appeared in my other books. At the same time many photos featured in this book have never appeared in print. I've been photographing rustic homes for more than thirty years now and have about one hundred thousand (give or take a few thousand) images in my personal library. Tragically, I did not record the owners of some of the homes I photographed years ago and am unable at this time to recall the builders, designers, masons or others involved in some of the projects. Please, if you recognize a home or fireplace that is not correctly acknowledged in this book please feel free to contact me at info@ralphkylloe.com. I will do my best to correct any misinformation.

As a rule I never say where a home is located or print the names of the homeowners. This usually works and no one has recently taken a shot at me. But to those whose homes appear here I want to personally thank each and every one of you. You know who you are and I thank you. At the same time I feel compelled to offer thanks to the following, including:

Harry Howard and Nicole Bates at Yellowstone Traditions, architect Larry Pearson, Alyssa Ruffie and Katie Lineberger at LPAIA, Jacque Spitler at Outlaw Design, Terry Winchell at Fighting Bear Antiques, Paul Shea, Curator of the Yellowstone Historic Center,

Melissa Greenaur, Diana Beattie, Robert and Liz Esperti, David and Christie Garrett, Chris Lohss, Barbara Collum, Margaret Grade, Architect Kirk Michaels, Architect Janet Jarvis, Robin and Tony Williams, Colt and Kathy Bagley, Heidi Weiskopf, Adam O'dell, Pinky O'dell, Cherly Gallinger, Bill and Wendy Nolan, Suzanne Novik, Tim Groth, Raj and Laura Keswani, Reed Crosby, Brent McGregor, Peter Winter, Angel Sandoval, Guy Fairchild, Phil Cox, Gary Gloyne, Mark Hanson, Jerry McCollum, Andrew Varela, Reed Crosby, Mike Riley at OSM, Bill Keshishian, and John Simpson.

As always I want to thank Madge Baird, my editor, Gibbs Smith, my publisher, and Christopher Robbins, CEO at Gibbs Smith, Publisher. My wonderful wife, Michele, has styled many of the photos in this book and is invaluable to my ongoing efforts. Thank you to my daughter, Lindsey, for her help with the settings and Tina and John Keller for their continuing efforts to make my life easier.

It's evening now and the leaves on the hardwood trees outside my windows are a vibrant red. Actually, their color is more of a rich rust hue than a traditional red. In truth, words and labels mean very little when it comes to describing colors. Words often fail to represent many things. Autumn is more of a state of mind than an actual time. It is a portent of things to come, a poke in the ribs. It is a wake–up call of the inevitable. It's also stunning and romantic.

I spent the afternoon stacking wood. A kindly gentleman in a red plaid jacket delivered a cord of wood to me in the morning. His grandson help unload the old Chevy truck that had served them well for many years. I paid the old man with a check and gave the ten-year-old boy a five-dollar tip for his help. The boy did not say "thank you." His smile was enough for me.

I wore old leather gloves as I stacked the wood. I also wore my heavy work boots, because years earlier I had dropped a large log on my foot, breaking a few toes! Ouch! My three cats played under my feet this afternoon as I struggled with armfuls of dry logs. The leaves fell gracefully from the trees in our yard, and I told my seven-year-old daughter that if she could catch a falling leaf before it hit the ground, the tree fairy would grant her one wish! She spent an hour chasing the leaves as sudden flutters of wind kept them from her grasp. Dried leaves, leaves that made oxygen from the carbon dioxide we exhaled, crackled under the weight of my feet. The leaves will never know how much I appreciate their efforts to keep all humanity alive. And the very trees on which they live are surely gifts from the gods! Superb in both form and freedom, they inflame the imagination with their strength and beauty.

I've always found peace in trees. True, forests are violent places and roots and branches fight horrific battles to grow; I, nonetheless, thrill in the calmness that, to my eyes, resides there.

Forests are homes to elves and druids. The mysteries of the shadows stir my imagination. And the sway and dance of the trees in motion brings new meaning to the term life.

On my back porch I stack a number of different types of wood, each species and each piece a marvel of creation and evolution. The freedom in nature and in wood thrills me. The gnarls and knots and twists and turns inherent in trees speak of pure freedom. Organic in every way, trees do whatever is necessary to survive. Of a hundred thousand acorns that hit the ground, maybe only one will flourish. The rest will feed untold squirrels, porcupines, chipmunks and other creatures whose lives and emotions we will never know. And if not consumed by such creatures, the seeds decompose and add their nutrients to the ground, only to be recycled again and again. It is the way of the world.

By evening my job is complete. From the back porch I bring in a pile of kindling. On my knees, I open the flue of my fireplace and grimace at the dust that collected in the chimney over the summer. On the grate I first stack some old papers and then small and larger pieces of scrap wood culled from my workshop. They ignite immediately once I put a match to them. Minutes later I place a few pieces of bark-on birch on the fire. It, too, flames quickly. Birch is a "quick wood." Like many romances, it catches fire, roars hot for a few minutes and then, to the disappointment of all involved, quickly dies, soon to be forgotten. It was fun while it lasted.

I then place a few oak logs on the fire. Oak, on the other hand, is slow to catch. It takes its time. There is no hurry. Like a great marriage or romance, it burns warm and steady for its lifetime. It is easy to anthropomorphize on this stuff and place human symbolism on the things and events in our lives.

After dinner my family and I and our three cats sit on the couch in front of the fireplace. The fire glows warm. We say very little. My daughter falls asleep on my lap and the cats purr with contentment as my wife strokes each with her gentle hands.

The fire crackles and pops as the wood releases oxygen trapped in its cells. Like fireworks, sparks and embers shoot out in all directions. The flames dance and cast an eerie spell on each of us. Fire is beyond explanation. It mystifies and fires our imaginations. It is at the same time a numinous and an ethereal experience. Both captivated and enchanted, we can easily gaze for long hours at flames in the hearth.

The smell of the flames permeates our home and the warmth of the fire brings comfort to us. It is in front of a fire that we became humans. For billions of generations we have sat around flames and collected our thoughts. It is where we've told our stories and reflected on our lives. It is there where romances were sparked and then endured. We sat around fires to keep us warm and to protect us from beasts of all sorts. It is the fireplace that has been the center of life throughout all humanity.

And so the fire burns down in my cabin. The cats eat the last morsels from their bowls and I carry my daughter to her room. I place the now empty wine glasses in the sink and promise my wife I'll wash them first thing in the morning. I stoke the fire one last time and pull the fire screen tight to insure that any final embers stay where they are supposed to. The scent from the fireplace lingers and the final glow from the fire sends a warm hue across the room as I turn off the remaining light. It's been a good evening.

CHAPTER ONE

Traditional Fireplaces

After the big bang, hydrogen atoms were caught in stellar whirlpools and compressed into huge balls. The enormous weight of the material caused nuclear fusion to happen. In time, all sorts of elements were created inside many suns. When the fuel inside a few of the suns ran out, they exploded, hurling chunks of rock in all directions. And from these stones earth people created some pretty cool fireplaces! Here are a few examples.

"You are a king by your own fireside,
as much as any monarch in his throne."

— MIGUEL DE CERVANTES
from Don Quixote de la Mancha

Facing: The home was designed by architect Larry Pearson and the fireplace was designed by Diana Beattie. Rod Cranford of North Shore Stone Works was the mason. Mined from quarries in Harlowton, Montana, the stone is called prairie moss rock. *Above left:* Built by the wizards at Yellowstone Traditions and designed by Architect Larry Pearson, this setting is actually a "members only" fishing camp on the shores of the Big Hole River in Montana. Trophy elk antlers are proudly displayed over the mantel. *Above right:* This classic western fireplace is complete with a mantel created from a recycled barn beam.

This small fireplace is located in one of the cabins at the Lake Placid Lodge, Lake Placid, New York. The two round logs that are holding up the mantel are referred to as corbels. As fireplaces age (this one was probably constructed in the 1930s), the stones often darken from creosote given off by flames that escape the firebox. The hickory furniture was designed by Ralph Kylloe.

Facing, above left: This fireplace was constructed by Rod Cranford of North Fork Stone Works. Stones found on the property were used to create the fireplace. *Facing, above right:* Andirons, fire screen and tolls by artist Glen Gilmore. Photo courtesy of Glen Gilmore.

Below left: On the shores of the Yellowstone River rests this small restacked building. Vertical, rectangular stones outline the upper edge of the firebox. The mantel is lodgepole pine. *Below right:* The walls of this home are six feet thick and can accommodate the more than ten feet of snow that often blankets this home. Located at nearly 9,000 feet above sea level, this structure houses several different fireplaces. Designed by architect Larry Pearson and constructed by mason Phil Cox, the fireplace was created from prairie moss rock.

This tapered fireplace has "battered" edges. The mantel is locally found rock. Objects such as moose mounts are hung by drilling a cement screw directly into the rock.

"A fire is nourished by its own ashes."

—LATIN PROVERB

Facing: This fireplace, designed by Larry Pearson and constructed by the rock wizards at Angel Sandoval Masonry, actually has three different fireboxes housed in one chimney system—two on the interior and one serving as an exterior fireplace on the deck. The home was constructed by Chris Lohss using recycled materials throughout. *Above:* This dry stack fireplace in a small cabin in the Yellowstone Club in Montana was built by Phil Cox of Big Sky Masonry. *Below:* Living room at the Lake Placid Lodge. Made in the 1930s from locally found stones, sadly the entire building was destroyed by fire in 2005.

Above left: Designed by architect Janet Jarvis, the home was constructed by Bashista Construction Company. The firm of Gallegos Masonry was the contractor. The chairs in the foreground were made by Doug Tedrow. *Above right:* This fireplace in a historic log cabin is darkened from years of use. It is positioned in the corner, as opposed to the more common center placement. *Below left:* Designed by Larry Pearson and created by Angel Sandoval, both the mantel and lintel are locally quarried stone. *Below right:* River rock, as seen in this fireplace, is often dug from the ground as contractors excavate the area in preparation for the foundation.

Rod Cranford of North Fork Stone Works created this fireplace in a small cabin
near the banks of the Yellowstone River. The cabin was designed and constructed
by the creative folks at Yellowstone Traditions from recycled materials.

This fireplace and home were designed by architect Augustus Shepard in 1919.
Sitting on the shores of a stunning lake in the Adirondack Park, the home is actually
a boathouse. A collection of antique hickory toy furniture sits on the mantel.

Left: This room is the Fisherman's Cabin at Manka's Inverness Lodge in Inverness, California, where the fireplace has comforted and warmed many guests throughout the years. It is complete with an impressive collection of rustic antiques and rustic furniture (acquired from the Ralph Kylloe Gallery). *Right:* The Alpine Lodge, on the shores of beautiful Lake George, offers cabins to vacationers. A massive bison head guards the setting. This building was originally created by the Tuttle Family in 1896 as an English Tudor mansion. It partially burned in the 1930s and was rebuilt by Joe Bergman as a log cabin resort at the end of that decade.

Left: Just west of Cody, Wyoming, sits this dude ranch. The sitting room in this 1920s ranch is complete with original antique western furnishings and cowboy memorabilia. The tapered fireplace (aka battered) was created from locally found field stone. *Right:* This setting rests off the shores of a small secluded lake in New Hampshire. The fireplace boasts a recessed compartment that doubles as viewing space for the owner's collection of small and large bronzes.

Left: This dining room is in a restaurant on the shores of Lake Okeechobee in southern Florida. Stuffed fish caught in the lake occupy the mantel and the surrounding walls of the restaurant.
Right: Designed by architect Kirk Michaels, Jim Baker of Northstar Masonry, Big Timber, Montana, created this fireplace from locally quarried field stone. The fireplace maintains an arched configuration over the firebox. Sturdy tree limbs were placed in the stones and serve as platforms for the cougar.

The recreation room of this New Hampshire home offers a stone fireplace with
elevated hearth and double corbels that support the stone mantel. Designed by
architect Chris Williams and constructed by White House Construction, the fireplace
was built by mason Ron Spooner.

This room is actually a stunning boathouse on a secluded lake in the Adirondacks.
The building was designed and constructed by architect Augustus Shepard in 1916.

"When such a time cometh
I do retire
Into an old room
Beside a bright fire:
O, pile a bright fire!"

—EDWARD FITZGERALD
"Old Song"

This stone fireplace contains a recessed log compartment, stone lintel and stone mantel. The stepped-back sitting stones add depth to the fireplace. Designed by Architect Larry Pearson, the fireplace was constructed by the masons at Sandoval Masonry. The home was constructed by OSM builders in Montana.

Above: Overlooking ponds and streams, this home offers a circular fireplace with radiating recycled barn beams. The sitting stones for the fireplace are of tumbled granite. Much of the stone for the walls and fireplace was recycled from an old building in Klamath Falls, Oregon. John Simpson was the contractor for the building. The mason for the building was Jerry McCollum of McCollum Masonry. *Facing:* This home and fireplace were designed by Architect Larry Pearson. Constructed of Harlow stone from Harlowton, Montana, three different masonry firms, including Guy Fairchild, Angel Sandoval and Phil Cox, contributed to the completion of the extensive stonework and numerous fireplaces within the home. The center vertical stone directly above the fire is called the keystone. Sitting stones around the fireplace provide viewing space for extensive collections of all forms of artwork. The home was masterfully built by the OSM company. See more of this home on pages 86–7.

Above left: Rancho Relaxo, designed by Larry Pearson and built by Bill Keshishian of Elephant Builders, rests on the shores of the mighty Yellowstone River. Dan Hanson was the mason. The complete fireplace system includes three fireboxes. *Above right:* This fireplace rests in a historical great camp in the Adirondacks. *Below left:* This fireplace offers "see-through" design. The fire can be enjoyed from both the living and dining room. The small mantel is lodgepole pine. *Below right:* We found this fireplace and its rustic furniture at an old fishing camp in Oregon, built in the 1920s.

Surrounded by Western and European antiques, this massive fireplace rests in a home
near the Grand Tetons in Wyoming. It was designed and created by builder Mike
Beauchemin; the stones came from a Rocky Mountain quarry.

This circular corner fireplace was constructed with Montana prairie moss rock.
Phil Cox was its designer and builder. Larry Pearson designed the home and
Yellowstone Traditions was the contractor.

"O, to have a little house!
To own the hearth and stool and all!"

—PADRAIC COLUM

Facing: This fireplace offers a recessed wood storage area under the raised hearth. Larry Pearson, architect; Ron Cranford, mason; Yellowstone Traditions, contractor; Dianna Beattie, interior designer. *Above left*: This fireplace occupies a second-floor master bedroom. Home designed by Larry Pearson; masonry and stonework throughout by Angel Sandoval, Phil Cox and Guy Fairchild. *Above right*: Home designed by Larry Pearson, built by Chris Lohss, *Below*: Architect Janet Jarvis, contractor Bashista Construction Company, mason Gallegos Masonry. The building rests on the Wood River in Ketchum, Idaho.

This home was designed by Architect Chris Williams and was built by White House Construction. The mason for the project was Ron Spooner. The chandelier was made by Dennis Sparlings of Middlebury, Vermont. The andirons are metal owls.

Above: This home and fireplace were designed and contracted by Peter Torrence of Torrence Construction, Lake Placid, New York. The stones are locally quarried granite. *Below:* This is another cabin at the Lake Placid Lodge. The building was created in the 1930s and was completely refurbished in the late 1990s. Furniture and interior design by Ralph Kylloe.

"I know the look of an apple that is roasting and sizzling on the hearth on a winter's evening . . ."

—MARK TWAIN

This library room was designed by Architect Larry Pearson and constructed by
Yellowstone Traditions. It rests in a gorgeous Cape Dutch building in Montana.
The wood paneling glows in the evening sun.

This office and fireplace rests in a great camp in the Adirondack Park.
The room and fireplace, constructed of locally found stone, were completed in
1999. Built-in bookcases and cabinets provide storage space for the owner's
extensive collections. The work desk is from the Ralph Kylloe Gallery.

Above left: This extensive stonework houses not only a fireplace but a TV as well. Designed by interior designer Heidi Weiskopf. *Above right:* This home sits outside of Jackson, Wyoming, within sight of the Yellowstone River. The mantel is a highly figured, burled lodgepole log. *Below left:* This fireplace was constructed by Adam O'Dell with stones that were dug on the property. A slab of thick white pine serves as the mantel. *Below right:* This towering fireplace sits in a home in New Hampshire. The cut canoe houses a TV and books.

Left: Scott Fuller Development completed this New Hampshire lakeside home. The fireplace fits nicely into a triangulated corner. Suzanne Novik was the interior decorator. *Right:* The firm of Gallinger/Trauner in Wilson, Wyoming, served as interior designer for this project. The floor-to-ceiling masonry contains a fireplace complete with western motif fire screen and a recessed wood storage area. A burled log is the mantel.

Above left: This small fireplace offers a fire screen adorned with handmade iron pinecones. A small, recycled barn beam serves as the mantel. *Above right:* A massive burled lodgepole pine tree serves as a mantel for this fireplace. *Below:* This outdoor, enclosed-porch fireplace was designed by Larry Pearson and constructed by Jamie Livingston. Yellowstone Traditions was the contractor for the project. The setting, complete with antique hickory furniture, overlooks a vast area of grasses, rivers, ponds and mountains.

Facing: Designed by architect Larry Pearson and the homeowner, this fireplace was constructed by Phil Cox of Big Sky Masonry of Montana prairie moss rock. *Above:* Another view of the Rancho Relaxo fireplace system. This fireplace faces the living room and was constructed by Dave Hanson. *Below left:* This tapered fireplace with an old barn beam as a mantel was also electrified to accommodate sconces. Home designed by Larry Pearson and constructed by Chris Lohss. *Below right:* Recycled materials were used to complete this high-elevation guest home. Chris Lohss, contractor; Angel Sandoval, mason; Larry Pearson, architect. Chandelier by Joe Holley.

Above: This western setting offers peeled-log furniture and a fireplace made from round river rocks. Red Native American rugs are often used in such settings to bring life and brightness to rooms. *Below:* Built in 1926, this fireplace rests in a small Adirondack Park boathouse complete with antique hickory furniture. One can jump off the front porch into a clear Adirondack lake!

This dry-stacked fireplace offers a fire screen adorned with custom-made
iron pine trees and other western icons. Traditional Molesworth-inspired
furniture fills the room.

This fireplace was constructed by Adam and Marvin O'Dell of Johnsberg, New York. The setting is Mr. Brown's Pub at the Sagamore Resort in Bolton Landing. Interior design and furniture by Ralph Kylloe.

Above left: Designed by architect Larry Pearson as a traditional alpine ski house, the home was built by Chris Lohss. Masons from Sandoval Masonry created the fireplace. *Above right:* This fireplace warms a large lakeside home in New Hampshire. Built from locally found stones, a slab of white pine serves as a mantel. *Below:* Built by Bob Waldron in Racquet Lake, New York, the home and fireplace rest on a lakeshore on an Adirondack lake. Antique hickory and Adirondack furniture provide seating for this porch setting.

"Go where he will, the wise man is at home,
His hearth the earth, his hall the azure dome."

—RALPH WALDO EMERSON
"Wood-notes"

This home rests on the shores of a large lake in northern Montana. Angel Sandoval
was the mason, Lenoch Builders constructed the home, and Larry Pearson was the
architect. Complete with original Arts and Crafts and hickory furniture, this view
shows the breezeway between the main home and the guesthouse.

CHAPTER TWO

Intimate Fireplaces

Arguably one of the most sensual and provocative elements in the world, fire stirs our imaginations. With its mysterious dance and warm glow, few things can excite the way fires can. Under the spell of a small, cozy fire, anything can happen.

"Announced by all the trumpets of the sky,

Arrives the snow, and, driving o'er the fields,

Seems nowhere to alight: the whited air

Hides hills and woods, the river, and the heaven,

And veils the farm-house at the garden's end.

The sled and traveller stopped, the courier's feet

Delayed, all friends shut out, the housemates sit

Around the radiant fireplace, enclosed

In a tumultuous privacy of storm."

—RALPH WALDO EMERSON
"The Snow-Storm"

Located on the shores of the Madison River in Montana, this small building
was created from recycled materials. The fireplace offers a flush hearth
that is even with the floor. Designed and constructed by Phil Cox of Big Sky
Masonry, the fireplace is created of prairie moss rock. The mantel is
made from lodgepole pine.

This fireplace occupies an entire wall of a very small cabin. Constructed by Rod Cranford of North Fork Stone Works, Placer mined river stones were used to create the structure. The small cabin, made from recycled materials, sits next to a great trout pond high in the Rockies.

Above left: The Crescent H Ranch in Jackson, Wyoming, built in the 1930s, is a hunting retreat that today hosts visitors and guests. The main hall, shown here, has two warming fireplaces. *Above right:* This modern ski resort condo in Vermont is given a rustic atmosphere with furnishings and accessories. *Below left:* A massive recycled barn beam functions as a mantel over this upstate New York fireplace. Armchair by Jonathan Sweet. *Below right:* This Montana bedroom fireplace is often lighted during the cold winter months. Created by Rod Cranford; architect, Candace Miller.

The asymmetrical geometric form of the fireplace is reminiscent of Cubism. The minimalist fireplace is complete with a glass fire screen.

Left: This fireplace is another example of a corner construction. Offering an elevated hearth, corbels and stone mantel, the fireplace blends well into the corner of this kitchen. *Right:* This bedroom fireplace offers a recessed area above the mantel and a dramatic keystone. Contemporary elk antler chairs add drama to the room. The home and fireplace were designed by Larry Pearson. Sandoval Masonry was responsible for the rockwork throughout the home.

This fireplace was designed by Larry Pearson. Brock Masonry was responsible for the
rockwork throughout the home. Harlowton stones were used throughout the home.
Candles are used in the firebox and add a romantic flair to the setting.

This is another example of a small, simple design for a fireplace. A glass fire screen protects the room carpet from flying embers. The arm chair in the foreground was made by Tim Groth.

CHAPTER THREE

Lodge Style Fireplaces

Lodges were initially manly places. Brazen and bold lodges spoke of strength and conquest. They were places to hang your trophies and get away from it all. Today lodges are often places where families gather, and it is in front of the fireplace where the great stories of our lives are relived and told.

—

"To the right, books; to the left,
a tea-cup. In front of me, the fireplace;
behind me, the post. There is no greater
happiness than this."

ANONYMOUS

This is a ground-level view of the fireplace at the Old Faithful Inn in Yellowstone
National Park. The fireplace is sixteen feet square at the base.

Facing: Architect Robert C. Reamer designed the Old Faithful Inn, which was completed between 1903 and 1904. The grand fireplace, constructed from rhyolite rock, stands 65 feet tall. *Above:* Just north of Yellowstone National Park sits this massive family structure complete with floor-to-ceiling fireplace. A matching fireplace sits at the other end of the great room. Home designed by Larry Pearson, constructed by Yellowstone Traditions, masonry overseen by Phil Cox.

This photo features the opposing fireplace in the grand hall of the home and room on the preceding page. *Facing, above left:* Built of Harlowton prairie moss rock, this fireplace features a flush hearth, large firebox and cascading height; Phil Cox, mason. *Facing, above right:* Mike Beauchemin constructed this large home, which houses the finest examples of original western and Native American furnishings and accessories.

Below left: This floor-to-ceiling fireplace features a fire screen by Glen Gilmore. Photo courtesy Glen Gilmore. *Below right:* This home was inspired by the "sourdough" cabins of the 1880s. Designed by Larry Pearson; constructed by Yellowstone Traditions; fireplace designed by Harry Howard of YT and built by Rod Cranford. Materials for the rockwork were found on the property.

"Mothers of our mother,
Foremothers strong.
Guide our hands in yours,
Remind us how
To kindle the hearth.
To keep it bright,
To preserve the flame.
Your hands upon ours,
Our hands within yours,
To kindle the light,
Both day and night."

—CELTIC BLESSING FOR HEARTH-KEEPERS

Three stories tall, this fireplace offers a massive stone lintel and hand-wrought fire screen, tools and andirons. Arts and Crafts Morris chairs and traditional western furniture complete the setting. More of this home is shown on pages 86 and 87.

Above and facing: In the town of West Yellowstone is a train station and dining hall that was completed in 1925. Architect Gilbert Stanley Underwood created the buildings for the Oregon Short Line Railroad. Eventually the rail company gave the historic buildings to the town of West Yellowstone and today they are used for offices, weddings and other activities. Rhyolite volcanic rock was used in the construction of the two fireplaces, acquired from both Wyoming and Ashton, Idaho.

The large fireplace (facing) was constructed in an arrowhead design. Massive in every way, it is large enough to walk inside (my wife and daughter are resting on the built-in sitting stones on the right). The large andirons, also in arrowhead design, are original to the setting. Paul Shea, historian for the town of West Yellowstone, informed me that Oliver C. Jones was the stone mason who stacked the fireplace. A small metal plaque on the fireplace reads: Oliver C. Jones, 1898–1957, Gentle-Caring-Outdoorsman.

A small fireplace on the opposite end of the building (above) is showing its age. Years of fires have darkened the stones directly above the firebox.

"Thank ye the gods, O dwellers in the land,
For home and hearth and ever-giving hand."

—DANIEL LEWIS DAWSON
"The Seeker in the Marshes"

The building that houses this fireplace is presently owned by the State of Colorado. Located near the town of Evergreen, Colorado, the fireplace was constructed with volcanic rock found in the local area. The whimsical andirons are modeled after long-necked birds. Much of the furniture in the building is Spanish influenced.

The three fireplaces shown above and facing are part of a fireplace system in one home. The mantel for the fireplaces above and facing above came from the bottom of the St. Lawrence Seaway. A piling for a dock/bridge system, solid oak and weighing over 7,000 pounds, was delivered to the job site and later cut in half. The layered fireplace facing above offers recessed seating areas on either side of the firebox. The rockwork was electrified to accommodate sconces. Architect, Larry Pearson; contractor, OSM; head mason, Phil Cox. *Facing, below:* Phil Cox at Big Sky Masonry completed this two-way fireplace. The chimney has two fireboxes, one in the kitchen and one in this dining room.

Facing: The architects for this project were Larry Pearson and YT Studios. Made from Harlowton prairie moss rock. Phil Cox of Big Sky Masonry constructed the fireplace. The tapered form, over-hangs on the mantel, arched keystone and cascading footings make this a classic fireplace. *Above:* A soft colored couch allows for relaxation in front of this "see-through" fireplace in Beaver Creek, Colorado. The short mantel is suspended by stone corbels.

"A crooked log makes a good fire."

—FRENCH PROVERB

This is another historic cabin at the Lake Placid Lodge in Lake Placid,
New York. Constructed in the 1930s, this fireplace offers a "bark-on"
mantel and top support beam.

Above: Four stone corbels were used to support the stone mantel on this fireplace.
Above left: This log home in the Catskill Mountains of New York was designed by
Maple Island Log Homes. The asymmetrical fireplace offers a stone mantel supported
by a single raised, vertical keystone. *Above right:* This room was created in 1921. The
owners who purchased it in the 1990s liked it so much that they built their new
home completely around the existing building. Mantel painting by Barney Bellinger.

Below left: Architect Kirk Michaels designed the home that rests on the shores of the Yellowstone River. John Baker of Northstar Masonry was the mason for the project.
Below right: Rod Cranford of Montana created this massive tall fireplace for a kids camp in Montana. Locally found rocks were used to construct the fireplace.

The mason for this superb fireplace was Jeff Madison. Designed by Larry Pearson
and constructed by Bill Keshishian, the home, aptly called Moose Meadows Ranch,
sits in a pleasant valley of the Bridger Mountains of Montana. The hammered
copper table lamp is by Michael Adams.

Left: A huge boulder serves as the keystone for this tall, tapered fireplace. Located in upstate Michigan, the stones for the fireplace were acquired on the property as the land was excavated for the foundation. *Right:* This geometric fireplace sits in a home in Idaho. The clean lines and well balanced form fit well into this contemporary home. The glass fire screen, with simple lines, complements the fireplace. The rustic chandelier was created by artist Randy Edgar of Bellevue, Idaho.

Above left: This fireplace was completed for interior designer Barbara Column by Paul Dudley. This home is located in a private camp in the Adirondack Park. *Above right:* This home was designed by architect Kirk Michaels. John Baker of Northstar Masonry was the mason for the project. Double corbels were used to support the log mantel. A bison head stands proudly over the fireplace. *Facing:* This is the original living room for Camp TopRidge. Regarded as the grandest of the Adirondack Great Camps, the compound was completed in the 1930s for Marjorie Merriweather Post. The room when I made this photo in the mid 1980s had sat untouched for many years. The furnishings and decorative accessories shown here are original to the home. The entire back wall, between the vertical posts comprised the grand fireplace for this hall. The "camp" was sold to a private individual in the 1990s, refurbished and redecorated. The home today still maintains its uniqueness and high style. For a complete photo essay on the compound please see my book *Adirondack Home.*

This huge fireplace graces the Oak Lodge in Pennsylvania. Made from locally found sandstone by mason Wade Thomas. The fireplace stands forty feet tall and is twenty feet wide. The fireplace maintains two recessed log holders and two more recessed compartments for collectibles. Reid Crosby, purveyor of fine wood for mantels, provided the massive burled maple tree for the mantel. Photo courtesy of Reid Crosby.

Above left: Created by Peter Torrence, this fireplace with level hearth sits in a kitchen in the Adirondack park. *Above right:* This setting features a corner fireplace, taxidermy and contemporary furniture. *Below left:* Located in Red Lodge, Montana, this corner fireplace includes a closed box wood stove. Such equipment provides warmth to supplement traditional heating systems. *Below right:* Made from local river rocks, this fireplace occupies an entire wall of the home.

CHAPTER FOUR

Sculptural and Organic

A great mason can make a fireplace come alive. Created with an artistic flair, great fireplaces can be full of movement and take on lives of their own.

"The carpet was up, the candles burnt bright, the fire blazed and crackled on the hearth, and merry voices and light–hearted laughter range through the room."

—CHARLES DICKENS
The Pickwick Papers

This enormous fireplace was created in 1953 by Earl Young for the Weathervane
Restaurant in Charlevoix, Michigan. The keystone is a 9-ton glacial boulder of
Michigan granite shaped almost exactly like Michigan's Lower Peninsula. Young was
a well-known developer/builder in the upstate Michigan area who created many
unique stone homes, cabins and fireplaces.

Facing: This corner fireplace in an Ohio home is a unique blend of stone and cement. *Above:* This fireplace in a B&B on Whidbey Island, Washington, was created from local beach rocks. A dramatic pine arch was incorporated into the design. *Below:* The owner of this home found a contorted tree on his property on the shores of the Yellowstone River and dragged it back to the ranch behind his horse. John Baker of North Star Masonry incorporated it into this bedroom fireplace.

Above: The massive stones used to assemble the fireplace were acquired from Pipe Stone Pass in Montana. Guy Fairchild constructed the fireplace and Larry Pearson served as architect for the project. A small sitting area inside the hearth allows one to cook marshmallows late at night! *Below:* Earl Young, of Charlevoix, Michigan, created this unique stone fireplace in a hotel lobby in Michigan. He has created many other unique stone fireplaces and cabins in the upper Michigan area.

This massive fireplace was created in the 1950s by Earl
Young, in upstate Michigan.

This unique home, located on the banks of the Beaverhead River in Montana,
includes numerous fireplaces. This triangular fireplace and others in the building
were created by Guy Fairchild. The stones for the structure were acquired from
Pipe Stone Pass in Montana. The architect for the project was Larry Pearson.
Yellowstone Traditions was the contractor.

"Keeper of the Hearth, kindle us.
Beneath your mantel, gather us,
And restore us to memory."

— *Celtic Blessing for Hearth-Keepers*

Facing: This fireplace was designed by Larry Pearson. The stones for the floor were salvaged from an old building foundation in Fort Klamath, Oregon. The mason for the project was Jerry McCollum. Old barn beams radiate out from the fireplace.
Above: This is another unique fireplace designed and constructed by Earl Young, Charlevoix, Michigan. Earl Young was a significant designer and developer in Charlevoix. He created Boulder Park, which featured many smaller cottages and homes created from locally found boulders and stones. He worked between the late 1930s and early 1960s.

Above and facing: This is actually a two-sided fireplace. Brent McGregor, from Sisters, Oregon, used highly figured, twisted juniper to create the mantels for the fireplaces.

Above: Brent McGregor created this amazing mantel and support structure from twisted juniper. The dead material is collected, sandblasted, sanded, and then applied to the structure of the fireplace. A further branch was added above the mantel for decorative purposes. *Facing:* This abobe brick and plaster-covered fireplace is an example of a traditional Southwestern design. Located in Wyoming, the setting is complete with cowboy boots, kachina dolls and Native American accessories.

This photo shows another cabin at the Lake Placid Lodge, Lake Placid, NY. The ornate mantel and overhead architectural applications were made from birch bark and locally found twigs and created by rustic artist Peter Winter.

Above left: This fireplace was completed for interior designer Barbara Column by mason Paul Dudley. Antler spikes surround a mirror that hangs on the fireplace. The home is in a private camp in the Adirondack Park. *Above right:* This fireplace was in the Lake Placid Lodge. The main building and this room and fireplace were destroyed in a fire in 2005. *Below:* This fireplace is part of the Lake McDonald Lodge in Glacier National Park, Montana. Created in 1913 by John Lewis as a hunting lodge, the facility contains historical hickory furniture and rustic memorabilia.

"Yesterday afternoon set in misty and cold. I had half a mind to spend it by my study fire, instead of wading through heath and mud to Wuthering Heights."

—EMILY BRONTË
Wuthering Heights

Created by White House Construction, this home sits on a quiet lake in New Hampshire. Ron Spooner was the mason for the project. A Barney Bellinger paint-ing rests above the fireplace mantel.

CHAPTER FIVE

Outdoor Fireplaces

Regardless of the time of year outdoor fireplaces bring families together and invoke such qualities that they become almost monuments of worship in themselves.

"Who loves the rain

And loves his home,

And looks on life with quiet eyes,

Him will I follow through the storm,

And at his hearth-fire keep me warm."

—FRANCES SHAW

This fireplace stands as both a skeleton and monument to better times past. The home that surrounded the fireplace burned to the ground in the 1950s.

Above: This tiered fireplace sits on the patio of a Spanish-influenced home in Tucson, Arizona. Local stones from the Catalina Mountains were used in the construction of the fireplace. Rod Cranford oversaw a number of local masons to complete the home. Architect, Larry Pearson. *Facing:* This outdoor fireplace was created by Guy Fairchild and Phil Cox. The home sits just north of Yellowstone National Park, and bears, cougars, elk and deer often wander though the grounds. Home designed by Larry Pearson, constructed by Yellowstone Traditions.

This home sits high in the mountains just south of Ennis, Montana. The fireplace
was constructed from placer-mined river stone by rock artist Rod Cranford.
Candace Miller was the architect for the home.

Above and below left: This setting is actually Manka's Inverness Lodge in Inverness, California. Manka's is arguably the finest rustic resort in California, offering five-star food and lodging. The exterior fireplace shown seems to have movement in itself and was created from locally found stones. The builder of the fireplaces for Manka's is Michael Eckerman. *Below right:* This chimney was created in the 1930s to warm a log cabin church within the Grand Teton National Park.

This fireplace is all that is left of a home that burned.

This outdoor fireplace extends the outdoor dining season when the weather turns cool.

CHAPTER SIX

Accessories

Fires need to be stirred and managed. And a creative artist can bring elements of profound design and craftsmanship to fireplace tools. The fireplace experience can be greatly enhanced with artistic fire screens, andirons and tools to keep the fire warm and bright.

"There is no place more delightful than one's own fireplace."

—MARCUS TULLIUS CICERO

This pair of andirons in the form of long-necked birds
was created in the 1930s.

Above: A close-up photo of the fireplace hardware used at the Old Faithful Inn in Yellowstone National Park. *Facing:* Custom fire screen with wildlife motif by Glen Gilmore. Photo courtesy of Glen Gilmore.

This hardware holder was created by rustic artist Brent McGregor of Sisters, Oregon.

Above: This pine tree fire screen and andirons rest in the old train station in West Yellowstone, Montana. Completed in 1928, the structure is today used by the town for offices and public events. *Below:* Fire screen by iron artist Glen Gilmore of Hamilton, Montana.

Two artistic fire screens created by Glen Gilmore. *Above:* A Native American theme is evident in the feather handles, arrow cross bars, and pseudo Navajo blanket design around the frame. *Below:* It's pheasant hunting season at this fireside. Photos courtesy of Glen Gilmore.

"Go fish and hunt far and wide day by day—farther and wider—and rest thee by many brooks and hearth-sides without misgiving."

—HENRY DAVID THOREAU
Walden

Above and facing: These two historical fire screens were found in dude ranches near the east entrance to Yellowstone National Park. They are still in use today and reflect traditional western influence.

Resources

Stone and Masonry

Alan Brock
Brock Masonry
P.O. Box 2418
Glenwood Springs, CO 81602
970.963.5500
alan@brockmasonry.com

Angel Sandoval Masonry
915 Jeanette, Apartment D
Belgrade, MT 59714
406.388.0863

Western Heritage Masonry
Guy Fairchild
P.O. Box 307
Clyde Park, MT 59018
406.686.9143

Big Sky Masonry
Phil Cox
505 N. 23rd Street
Bozeman, MT 59715
406.682.7862

Gary M. Gloyne
931 Deetz Rd.
Mt. Shasta, CA 96067
530.926.4418
blacksmith@finestplanet.com

Jerry McCollum
McCollum Masonry
877 Casino Rd.
Medford, OR 97501
541.779.3757
gmccollum541@charter.net

Mark Hanson
Bozeman, MT
406.587.3557

Set in Stone

Andrew Varela
P.O. Box 1525
Bozeman, MT 59771
406.582.7820

Builders

Blue Ribbon Builders
145 Center Lane Unit L, Meadow Village
P.O. Box 160068
Big Sky, MT 59716
406.995.4579
Fax: 406.995.4043
info@blueribbonbuilders.com

Yellowstone Traditions
34290 E. Frontage Rd.
Bozeman, MT 59715
406.587.0968

Architects

Candace Tillotson-Miller Architect, AIA
P.O. Box 470
208 West Park St.
Livingston, MT 59047
406.222.7057
www.ctmarchitects.com

Dan Joseph Architect
P.O. Box 4505
Bozeman, MT 59772
800.800.3935

Jarvis Group Architects
511 Sun Valley Rd., Ste. 202
P.O. Box 626
Ketchum, ID 83340
208.726.4031
www.jarvis-group.com

Jeff Thompson
220 South Ninth Ave.
Bozeman, Montana 59715
406.586.3553

KMA, Inc.
Kirk Michels Architects
409 East Callender St.
Livingston, MT 59047
406.222.8611
406.222.6520

LPAIA (Bigfork)
Adam Britt
836 Holt Dr., Ste. 308
Bigfork, MT 59911
406.837.0201

LPAIA
Larry Pearson
777 E Main St., Ste. 203
Bozeman, MT 59715
406.587.1997

Pond and Stream Consulting, Inc.
Alex T. Fox, EI
Resource Engineer
626 Ferguson Ave., Ste. 1
Bozeman, MT 59718
406.522.4056
Email alex@pondandstream.com

Blacksmiths/Iron Workers/ Lamp Builders

Chicken Coop Forge
992 East River Dr.
Lake Luzerne, NY 12846
518.798.9174
www.chickencoopforge.com

Glen Gilmore
Gilmore Metalsmithing Studio
P.O. Box 961
Hamilton, MT, 59840
406.961.1861

Joe Holley
360 Fortsville Rd.
Gansevoort, NY 12831
518.745.5702

Kevin Warren
Warren Welding
110 N D St.
Livingston, MT 59047
406.222.0583

Tile

Ceramica Specialty Tiles
406.582.8989

Furniture Builders

Diane Ross
Rustic Furniture Limited Company
P.O. Box 253
Willow Creek, MT 59760
406.285.6882
www.rusticfurniture.net

Doug Tedrow
Wood River Rustics
P.O. Box 3446
Ketchum, ID 83340
208.762.1442

Jimmy and Linda Covert
2007 Public St.
Cody, WY 82414
307.527.5964

Lester Santos
2102 Southfork St.
Cody, WY 82414
307.527.7972

Galleries

Fighting Bear Antiques
P.O. Box 3790
375 South Cache Dr.
Jackson, WY 83001
307.733.2669

Ralph Kylloe Gallery
P.O. Box 669
Lake George, NY 12845
518.696.4100
www.Ralphkylloe.com